THE
CYCLING
REVOLUTION

First published in Great Britain in 2021 by
Michael O'Mara Books Limited
9 Lion Yard
Tremadoc Road
London SW4 7NQ

Text © Patrick Field 2021
Illustrations © Harry Goldhawk 2021

A CIP catalogue record for this book is
available from the British Library.

Papers used by Michael O'Mara Books Limited are natural, recyclable products made from wood grown in sustainable forests. The manufacturing processes conform to the environmental regulations of the country of origin.

ISBN: 978-1-78929-330-2 in hardback print format
ISBN: 978-1-78929-331-9 in ebook format

1 2 3 4 5 6 7 8 9 10

Designed by Ana Bježančević
Printed and bound in China

www.mombooks.com

THE
CYCLING
REVOLUTION

Lessons from Life on Two Wheels

PATRICK FIELD
Illustrated by Harry Goldhawk

Michael O'Mara Books Limited

INTRODUCTION

LEARNING HOW TO RIDE A BIKE IS LEARNING HOW TO LIVE

There is no magic formula for learning how to ride a bike. As founder of the London School of Cycling, my aim is not to tell people what to do but to give them the knowledge and skills that will help them establish styles of riding that suit their needs. New reasons for cycling and bike travel keep popping up, while excuses not to, weaken and fade.

Enjoyable cycling requires confidence and skill so, in many ways, learning how to ride is learning how to live. The hardest part of any bicycle journey is the idea, and getting the pedals turning is a triumph of will. Determination will take you the rest of the way.

In the two centuries since the bike's invention, there have been many 'bibles' and 'handbooks' explaining how to ride. This is not another. It won't tell you what you must or mustn't do: my aim is to help you work out how to use bicycles to make your life more convenient, satisfying and beautiful.

This little book of principles and parables won't give you answers to life, but I hope it will help you puzzle your way towards them. Better cycling is a bonus.

GREAT WORK CAN BE ITS OWN REWARD

On 12 June 1817, Baron Karl Friedrich Drais von Sauerbronn rolled his wood and iron running machine 14 kilometres (9 miles) along the best road in Baden, from Mannheim to Rheinau and back, the first documented two-wheel ride. Subsequent bicycle development is, by comparison, mere refinement.

In 1848, the 'year of revolutions', Drais renounced his title in sympathy. In authoritarian times, a baron turned democrat was not a figure to be celebrated. Citizen Karl, as he now styled himself, was stripped of his pension and died poor. France and Britain produced their own national pretenders to the title 'Father of the bicycle'. The 1917 centenary, which might have reminded the world of Karl's genius, fell during the Great War.

In 2017, a jolly weekend festival in Mannheim provided a low-key start to bicycling's third century. Ride from central Mannheim to Rheinau today and you will pass the unlovely suburb of Neckarau – the home of Germany's biggest bike shop. Maybe this would be enough for modest Karl Drais? Great work can be its own reward, after all.

ONLY CHANGE IS RELIABLE

Riding a bike is falling. The breakthrough is discovering that you can carry on falling without ever falling down. This is often called 'learning to balance'; more precisely, it's getting used to *not* being balanced – becoming comfortable in a dynamic state where only the forces are balanced.

A bike falls left or right. By steering the front wheel while rolling ahead, a rider moves their points of contact with the ground sideways, as well as forward. This switches the direction of their fall, converting falling in one direction into wobbling between two. The speed of this sideways movement is proportional to the rate of forward progress, which explains why riding slowly requires more finesse than going faster.

Nothing stays the same. In geological time, continents drift; in historical time, cities are washed away. Now, change accelerates at a bewildering pace. The two-wheeler was a key engine in the development of modernism. Its continuous instability is also a perfect metaphor for today's world – only change is reliable.

SAVOUR YOUR TRAVELS

A cyclist travels slowly enough to study the landscape in detail. Scents and sounds are there to savour. Greetings can be exchanged with anyone you pass. A bicycle is sufficient property for you to appear respectable; not enough to make you unapproachable. It's also somewhere to hang your luggage.

On a bike, you're as present in the landscape as any traveller on foot. The addition of wheels exaggerates the contrast between up and down, so you feel and remember the contours better: climbing from cornfields, through woods, up to rocks and snow, crossing from one river system to the next, broaching a pass to descend to where people speak in a new accent or language.

All these transitions happen faster and with more immediacy on two wheels: contrasting intimate close-ups with patterns visible from space. If we're meant to walk, why have we been given bicycles?

QUESTION RECEIVED WISDOM

In 1868, George Routledge and Sons published *Velocipedes, Bicycles, and Tricycles: How to Make and How to Use Them.* In it, the anonymous author confidently claims, 'The experience of all velocipedists points to a large driving-wheel in front as the best and easiest to work.'

Nobody is born knowing how to ride a bicycle, so 'how-to' handbooks certainly have their place. Problems come with definitive claims. At least the sage of 1868 was happy to admit his advocacy for front-wheel drive was based on hearsay. Today, 'truths' are more probably derived from marketing hype or the kind of bar-room lore favoured by men who prefer talking knowledgeably about bikes to riding them.

Following a beaten path is always easier than cutting your own. It's prudent to begin by following the ways of others. But as your experience grows, be prepared to make deviations. Maybe front-wheel drive is set for a comeback?

GO BEYOND YOUR COMFORT ZONE

Entering a non-competitive time trial, or randonnée, is agreeing to cover a route within a set number of hours. You can fail by abandoning or missing the time limit. Everyone who doesn't fail is a winner. Notable examples are the Paris–Brest–Paris and London–Edinburgh–London.

Every outbound descent will be a climb on the road home. This produces a nagging sense of being in a hole and digging deeper. The 'turn' is the glorious moment when you stop making your situation worse and start to self-rescue. Stopping above the Atlantic at Brest, with 600 kilometres (370 miles) in your legs, is like taking pictures on top of Everest, a heady moment to be relished, aware that the job is half done.

You can extend the principle to any trip that goes beyond your comfort zone. A spin to the seaside or mission to visit your in-laws can be a test of power, technical control and fortitude – a vehicle for personal growth.

10,000 X 0 = 0

There are trips so short they make no demands. Does the bike have air in the tyres? Does the time saved by riding instead of walking justify the trouble of getting it out? Answer 'yes' to both, swing your leg over and spin away – a 'nothing' journey.

Other outings require thought. Have I got clothes for the weather? Have I eaten enough? Do I know where I'm going? Will I need lights? Good preparation is key to successful travel. But don't get bogged down by the idea.

When setting off to go far, think first of a 'nothing' trip – the ride to the first river crossing, first hilltop or important junction. Don't mortify yourself with the thought of tens, hundreds or thousands of kilometres. A long journey is also a sequence of short ones. Solve the technical problems that are in front of you and consider the simple equation: $10,000 \times 0 = 0$.

GOOD PEOPLE ARE EVERYWHERE

In April 1884, Thomas Stevens departed San Francisco intent on circumnavigating the world – a bicycling first. He crossed North America then, in the following summer, he went across England, Europe, Turkey and Iraq before resting for the second winter in Tehran.

In 1886, he was detained in the closed country of Afghanistan and escorted back to Iran. Returning to Istanbul, he sailed for India and wheeled from Lahore (now in Pakistan) to Calcutta. Finally, after another sea trip, he crossed eastern China, then Japan, reaching Yokohama in December 1886.

His state-of-the-art 'Columbia Expert' – the type of machine later derided as a 'penny-farthing' – weighed over 20 kilograms (44 pounds). His journal features plenty of scrambling on rough paths, using his high bicycle to 'pole-vault' unbridged streams, races with horses and many problems with local officials unsure of what to do with the futuristic foreigner. Yet, while Stevens carried a revolver on his travels, unsurprisingly he never needed to use it in anger. His prejudiced 'imperial' attitudes were tempered by good humour and intrepid curiosity. Good people are everywhere; it's our preconceptions that need to change.

OWN THE ROAD

I t takes boldness to begin cycling on busy roads. This leads many people to mistake traffic riding for a 'warrior' skill. The primary dangers come from the actions of others, so being safe and comfortable requires communication, empathy and the ability to resolve any antagonism with minimum stress.

What's needed is confident tolerance. At times, your plans will conflict with the intentions of others, but that doesn't make them your enemies. The default attitude is, 'Yes, I do own the road. Let's share it.' Everyone on the road has the same basic status: that of a human being.

Learning to be calm, comfortable and authoritative while dealing with random strangers who are controlling hundreds of times more power than you is personal growth. Riding a bike is good for your heart and lungs. On busy roads, it's also free assertion training.

DON'T REJECT IDEAS JUST BECAUSE THEY'RE CRAZY

In the 1880s, a road was bare earth or maybe a load of stones. A tyre was an iron hoop shrunk around a wooden wheel. Placing a rubber bag, inflated with compressed air, between wheel and road was clearly preposterous. Arthur du Cros of the Dunlop Company described how his first journey through the streets of London on air tyres 'moved the sober citizens to mirth'.

The value of this technology was later proved by racing success. In 1891, Charles Terront, riding a Humber bicycle shod with Michelin pneumatic tyres, won the first Paris–Brest–Paris race, covering 1,196 kilometres (743 miles) in 71 hours 22 minutes – an event that signals the start of the modern age. It inspired the Paris–Brest, a commemorative dessert comprising a hollow ring of choux pastry filled with sweetened cream flavoured with hazelnuts. Don't knock something until you've tried it.

THERE IS NO FREEDOM WITHOUT FREEDOM OF MOVEMENT

In the mid-nineteenth century, women were largely excluded from public life and constrained by rigid social rules and dress codes. Until 1890, the only respectable option for the aspirational female cyclist was a tricycle, which allowed sedate pedalling in a long, full skirt.

The 'safety bike' was conceived as a niche alternative to the simpler high-wheeler, and its chain drive and pneumatic tyres made it more democratic. The boom of the 1890s brought its price within reach of any skilled worker.

Once shod with air tyres, the 'safety' became *the* bicycle and sent the 'penny-farthing' to the museum. The safety's popularity was partly driven by its appeal to women of all classes. The rational dress movement predated the bicycle; the boom supercharged it. Fashionable and modern, the bicycle was incompatible with tight-laced corsets. Sporty riding encouraged the use of divided skirts or baggy britches. The bicycle's respectability was confirmed by its use by clergymen's wives and daughters, and it allowed well-bred ladies to travel without a chaperone.

OPEN YOUR MIND TO POSSIBILITY

On an 1892 New England night ride, Hiram Maxim had the fancy of fitting an engine to his bicycle, unaware that, in 1886 in Mannheim, Germany, Karl Benz had already run a gasoline-powered tricycle. Maxim made an engine and mounted it on an old tandem trike. Headhunted by Pope Manufacturing, America's largest bicycle works, he engineered motorized tricycles and four-wheelers. Battery power was favoured by manufacturers, who imagined normal people would never master a clutch and gearbox. Maxim always preferred gasoline – noisy, dangerous, hard to tame – but widely available at paint shops or drugstores, giving access to the wild, open road.

In later life, Maxim explained that the simultaneous, independent, worldwide emergence of 'horseless-carriage' experimenters wasn't triggered by the advent of the gasoline engine – steam power could have been used decades earlier. Before 1885, they'd all been satisfied with walking, horses and the railways. It took the bicycle to free their minds.

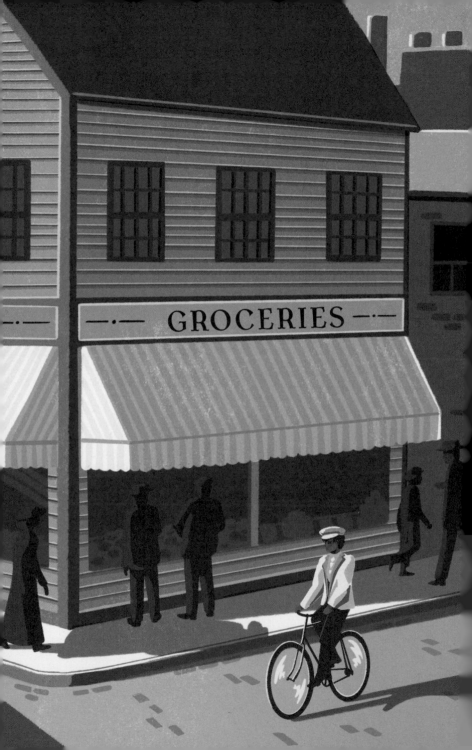

DON'T BE AFRAID OF CONTROVERSY

The League of American Wheelmen was founded in 1880, the era of the 'high bicycle', when cycling was restricted to rich, daring men. In 1893, a nineteen-year-old Boston seamstress, Katherine 'Kittie' Knox, joined the league. An accomplished and speedy rider, Knox was bold enough to design, manufacture and wear a knickerbocker riding suit, at a time when women in trousers scandalized polite society.

In 1894, the league resolved that 'none but white persons can become members'. Kitty, a woman of colour, attended the 1895 annual meet in New Jersey, showed her membership card and asked for entry. The resulting controversy drew national attention but the 'colour bar' was upheld. The league disintegrated in 1902. Revived and renamed the League of American Bicyclists, the prohibition was formally rescinded in 1999.

ENJOY FLYING, PRACTISE LANDING

Riding a bike gets easier the faster you travel – until you panic. To relax at speed and avoid danger, it's prudent to practise stopping. The brakes slow the wheels. The wheels' grip on the ground slows the bike. This grip is enabled by 'downforce', which mostly comes from the rider.

Slowing down transfers weight from the back wheel onto the front. The rider needs to push their weight backwards to keep the rear wheel down. What stops the bike is the rider; what stops the rider is the bike.

If a panicky rider gets off too soon, they meet the ground while still moving, relying on the animal quickness of their feet to keep them upright. Meanwhile, the unweighted bike becomes a flying hazard. This can end badly.

Rapid stopping requires the rider to stay in full, five-point contact with the bike. Once they are completely still there's plenty of time to get off or ride away. Dare to fly – but learn how to stop first.

THE PAST IS A DIFFERENT COUNTRY

From the start, bicycle racing focused on promoting and selling bicycles, bike components and newspapers. Records excited the public. Top professionals kept teams of pacemakers who, to go faster, rode tandems, triplets, quads and quints. As speeds increased, the multi-cycles reached a limit; adding more riders didn't help. Spectators of the late 1890s heard would-be record-breakers screaming 'more pace' behind their gasping windbreakers. In 1899, Charles 'mile-a-minute' Murphy rode 1,600 metres (1,760 yards) in fifty-seven seconds behind a specially adapted train on the Long Island railroad – a potentially deadly, unrepeated feat.

Racing cyclists needed to be paced. Motorcycles had become the only option. For ten years, the demands of record-breaking cyclists accelerated the development of fast, reliable motor vehicles. Later, the 'humble' bicycle was considered as some kind of alternative to motorcycles, automobiles and aircraft. In fact, it was their spark.

CONTROL IS CRUCIAL

The Wright brothers' aviation experiments were financed by profits from their store-front bike works. In winter, when the shop was quiet, they'd travel to North Carolina's secluded Outer Banks, where the sea breeze was reliable and dunes provided soft landing.

Other would-be flyers had worked on motorcycles and automobiles. Focused on power, they were constructing winged rockets capable of short hops, more like a stunt motorcyclist jumping a rank of buses than an aircraft. The Wrights used a single-cylinder gasoline engine to power machine tools in their shop. They'd worked with printing presses but never on powered vehicles. They studied birds and used a rig mounted on a bicycle's handlebars to test various wing sections. They built a wind tunnel. Starting with big kites, they moved on to gliders with adjustable wings. When they could control these, they put a rudimentary engine in an aeroplane and, for the first time in history, flew it successfully.

Power can be useful, but control is crucial.

BREAK DOWN BARRIERS

Marshall W. 'Major' Taylor from Indianapolis burst into the roughhouse world of 1890s track racing like an explosive shell: very young, very fast and very black. Crowds loved him and established champions and promoters mostly welcomed his popularity. 'Cheap professionals', however, had a problem, taking every chance to hinder his progress on, and off, the track and interpreting his modest politeness as 'uppity'.

Slightly built, to avoid being jostled and boxed-in, he raced from the front, increasing his fan appeal. In 1898, aged twenty, he was denied an opportunity to become national champion by bans preventing him entering rounds held in the American South.

Against the clock, freed from racist chicanery, Taylor proved his powers. In August 1899, he covered a motor-paced, flying-start mile in 1 minute 22.4 seconds, a new world record at almost 70 kilometres (43 miles) per hour. 'The fastest cyclist in the world' competed against champions in Europe and Australia – the first African-American global superstar.

THE WATCH DOESN'T LIE

The classic safety bike design is often cited as unimprovable. It's simple, versatile and robust. There are, however, political reasons, as well as engineering and ergonomic ones, for its dominance.

In 1933, riding a recumbent bike, Francis Faure broke the hour record by half a mile. 'The hour' is a totemic velodrome event, which measures the distance covered in sixty minutes from a standing start. The little-known Faure relied on the aerodynamic advantage of his laid-back, horizontal recumbent position. In 1934, the Union Cycliste Internationale (UCI) banned his bike and began making rules concerning what a bicycle *should* look like. Without these rules, time-trial bikes would be very different.

The current, UCI-approved men's hour record is 55.09 kilometres (34.23 miles); the recumbent record is 92.43 (57.43 miles). Restricting what's used in races encourages the idea that bicycles are old-fashioned.

Bikes do retro very well, but most people don't expect to solve modern problems with nineteenth-century machines.

KNOW WHICH WAY THE WIND BLOWS

Y ou can trust hills. Ride up one and, later, you can ride down it. Wind is less reliable. You may struggle in a block headwind for hours, stop for coffee and find it's died off and won't push you home. Beginners may mistake a tailwind for good form, go out too far and grovel coming back.

Of the forces that slow a rider down, only atmospheric resistance rises exponentially with speed through the air. If you ride fast, it's always windy, and small increases in speed require big increases in power. Casual riders mostly notice atmospheric resistance in high winds, when it's best to eschew flappy clothes. In microclimates, among cliffs or tall buildings, watch the swirling patterns of litter on the road ahead to prepare for gusts that can blow you sideways.

It may seem quaint to study the movement of air like an old-time sea captain but, even today, when the wind changes at an airport they turn the planes around to increase safety and save money. Cycle travel puts you in direct contact with the physical realities of the world.

GET MOVING, THEN FIND YOUR PURPOSE

Gino Bartali won the Giro d'Italia twice in the 1930s and the Tour de France in 1938. Conscripted into the army in 1940, Italy's number-one sportsman wasn't sent abroad to fight. Instead, he delivered military messages on home soil, allowed to use a bike rather than a motor-scooter.

When the Fascist government of Italy collapsed, Italy's German allies became an army of occupation, leaving Italian Jews, already persecuted by Fascists, even more vulnerable to deportation and murder.

Bartali dropped out of the army and was recruited by a secret network. Unaffected by fuel shortages, able to dodge mobile patrols, he rode thousands of kilometres delivering forged identity documents for Jews. His fame provided some protection, 'training for his profession' an alibi, but, in a time of violent chaos, it was dangerous work.

After the war, he never talked about these missions, not wanting his fame to overshadow the greater suffering and sacrifices of others. People with bikes are hard to govern and harder to oppress.

LIFE IS NOT A
POPULARITY CONTEST

○○○

Part of being safe while cycling amongst other traffic is making other people think about you. You don't need to be pushy but making them consciously aware of your presence is essential.

Obviously, you're not in control of how others react when they think about you. Maybe they'll admire your shoes? If they're not on their bike they might feel inspired to go for a ride later, or they may be enraged by envy? No matter, if they're thinking about you, you're safe.

Popularity can warm your heart and help you get what you want. But being visible and being fully seen is essential to life on two wheels. The more accomplished you become at controlling the space around you and finding your place on the road, the easier it gets to be safe and popular. If you have to choose between popular *and* safe, which would you prefer?

CHALLENGE STEREOTYPES

⊙ ⊛ ⊙

'**P**at Hanlon' was the neutral name above the shop window. Some customers knew exactly who the white-haired woman in a blue nylon overall was. She'd moved to London forty years earlier and worked as a waitress. She had started racing, with promise, and went to Macleans 'Featherweights' in Islington for a new machine. She'd always done her own maintenance and started hanging round the shop looking to be useful. A female mechanic was not necessarily a popular concept in those days.

The Second World War meant a shortage of male labour, so Pat learned her métier – wheel-building – with Macleans, and was acknowledged as the best of her time. Top professionals from all over Europe, hard-riding tourists and discerning club riders beat a path to her door.

Check your generalizations and stereotypes. The men who refused Pat's wheels missed riding hoops built by the hands that laced, tightened and trued the ones that – for example – carried Rik Van Looy over the cobbles to win Paris–Roubaix in 1965. She closed the shop in 1983 and retired to Majorca to ride her bike.

FITNESS AND HEALTH ARE NOT THE SAME

Fausto Coppi and Gino Bartali are linked forever as rivals. Teak-tough, Bartali prayed faithfully, drank wine, smoked tobacco and battered his opponents with relentless attacks. Six years younger, Coppi pioneered team tactics, spoke Italian, French, Flemish and English, and – more than anyone else – invented modern road-racing. Nervous and fragile, prone to broken bones and stomach upsets, he could judge when to make a single decisive attack. Once clear, he had uncatchable speed.

Coppi used the best mechanics and masseurs, drank fruit juice and ate raw vegetables, yogurt, wheatgerm and grilled meat. His scientific pursuit of fitness led him to amphetamine, which wasn't banned or frowned upon in the 1940s and 1950s. He relied on it during his years of dominance and decline. He died, worn-out, early in 1960, aged forty. Taken to extremes, fitness is not healthy.

Bartali lived into old age as a grumpy celebrity. He is remembered fondly. Fausto Coppi is venerated as a legend.

BAD ROADS ARE GOOD

A highlight of a 1950s tour of Scotland was storming the Lairig Ghru, a remote Highland pass connecting Braemar, on the River Dee, with Aviemore, in the valley of the Spey.

It's 100 kilometres (62 miles) from Aviemore to Braemar on paved roads, or 40 via the Lairig Ghru. Before the coming of the railways, when the pass was a thoroughfare for people on foot, horseback or driving animals, community effort went into keeping the path free from fallen rocks. While other, lower routes have now been improved, the Lairig Ghru gets rougher over time.

The route is mostly forest tracks or dusty estate roads, but the highest section is a boulder field where even pushing a bike is impossible. There are streams to be forded. Hardy tourists wouldn't have described it as 'off-road', more probably they would have called it 'a bit of rough stuff'. Bad roads, impassable to less flexible traffic, often connect long, quiet routes that are no through roads for most motor traffic. They can provide a more direct route and a gruelling test that makes arriving all the sweeter.

ENJOY YOUR LIFE NOW

If Beryl Burton had been French, Joan of Arc would have had to take second place. World champion on road and track, prolific winner of time trials and mass-start races, Burton won her first national title in 1958 and her last in 1983. All this was achieved while working full-time, raising a child and financing her own racing. After being feted as a superstar in Italy, Germany or the Netherlands, she'd get off a train in Leeds and appear to be just an odd lass walking home with two bikes and a bag.

Fiercely competitive, Beryl lost count of her medals. Winning was the satisfaction of an objective attained, not something to gloat over; the prime motivation of her career was always the pleasure of cycling. She could usually remember what she was given to eat after an important race while the event itself was often forgotten. Focus shifted to the next challenge; crashes, defeat, victory and injuries slipped into the background.

Plan for the future. Remember the best of the past. And enjoy your life now.

KNOW THE DIFFERENCE BETWEEN REHEARSAL AND PERFORMANCE

◦ ◉ ◉ ◉

An early-season, midweek race in Flanders. Eddy 'the Cannibal' Merckx, the most successful bike-racer in history, spins along anonymously in the semi-vacuum created at the centre of a moving pack. He's wearing long tights and is not riding to win or to engineer a victory for one of his loyal teammates.

There's a distinction between 'rehearsal' and 'performance' or, to put it another way, 'out for a ride' and 'travelling somewhere'. When you're out for a ride, there's no need to conserve energy. You can try anything: untested routes, new equipment, or practise new skills. You can ride so hard you come home a ghostly wreck, extending capacity through physical stress followed by rest and recovery.

It's sometimes necessary to take risks in performance. These uncertainties can be reduced by good work and experimentation in more playful times.

In Flanders, at the finish, as riders peel off their clothes, one or two notice that the Cannibal has ridden 190 kilometres (120 miles) with weights strapped to his ankles.

BEWARE SIMPLE ANSWERS

How hard shall I pump the tyres? Hitting a bump with tyres too soft results in a compression puncture, two symmetrical 'snake-bite' holes in the tube. The narrower the tyres, the harder they need to be to prevent this. Tyres pumped harder are rounder and roll better.

Pneumatic tyres work by keeping you on the ground when you hit a bump. If you leave the ground even for a quarter a second, you slow down. On smooth roads, your tyres can be hard. Softer tyres suit bumpier ground.

If the rider, bike and luggage, are heavy, the tyres can be hard. Where this load is lighter the tyres can be softer. Depending how the load is distributed, the tyres needn't be exactly the same pressure.

Finally, how dynamic is the rider? If she uses her arms and legs as active suspension, pressing the bike on the road, the tyres can be harder than if she sits passively and lets the bike bounce. Simple questions are many; simple answers fewer.

REST WHEN IT'S EASY

◌ ⊙ ◌

On the flat, it's possible to keep up with others by rolling along in the turbulent air behind them. Going uphill, the workload increases and the benefit of such sheltering goes down, assuming speed drops. It's like sea bathing: when the tide goes out, you discover who is swimming naked.

Alone, or with a group committed to keeping together, you can climb at a comfortable pace, changing down through the gears to maintain an even power output. But don't ease off at the top – accelerating back to cruising speed is the most critical part of the climb. Go uphill as slowly as necessary but keep pushing as the road levels out. Then you can take a break while moving fast.

If you want to rest while walking, you have to stop and find somewhere to sit down. On a bike, you're already sitting down and can rest while breezing along, assuming the luxury of a freewheel.

JUST RIDE

In a booth behind the Shimano stand at an autumn trade show in Milan, reigning world road race champion Gianni Bugno was struggling. He rode for an Italian team whose bikes carried Japanese equipment, a novelty in the early 1990s. In the preceding season, he'd used the new Shimano Total Integration (STI) system. STI allows the rider to change gear without taking their hand off the brake lever.

On some days, Bugno had ridden a bike with STI levers, on others he'd reverted to gear levers on the down tube. A journalist was grilling him on the choice. Was it to do with weight, ergonomics, terrain? Bugno, only in the cramped, noisy cubicle to fulfil contractual obligations, was careful not to say anything that could be misinterpreted as criticism.

Finally, he drew the line of questioning to an emphatic close: 'I ride whatever the mechanic hands me in the morning.'

The specification of your bike will always be a compromise. Just ride it.

LEARN FROM
YOUR MISTAKES

Josie Dew, young and alone, pedalled slowly up a Swiss mountain pass. The sun set and a chill, wet mist rolled in with the creeping darkness. The fog thickened, her headlight hardly penetrating the eerie gloom. Only occasional white-washed rocks along the roadside lay between Josie and a long, long drop. She needed to find somewhere to sleep soon. In a small lay-by just before a tunnel, she made out a workman's hut. Forcing a boarded window, she clambered through with her bags, then her bike, to sleep on a table while a howling storm rocked the shed.

As the peaks glistened in a cold, perfectly clear morning, Josie noticed the hut was perched on the very edge of a precipice, with three of its four anchoring stays snapped. She'd been depending on one frayed wire all night, and resolved, regardless of desperation or fatigue, to check future accommodation more carefully.

Learn from your mistakes, if you survive them.

BE AN EXPERT ON YOUR OWN LIFE

The first time floating on two wheels, or riding for a whole day or a whole night – any trip that goes beyond a previous limit – can generate strong sensations. So strong that it's possible to mistake personal revelation for universal truth.

When somebody, almost certainly a man, says, 'This is how you must ride a bike,' what they invariably mean is, 'This is how I ride a bike and it works for me.' If they're efficient, their riding gives them satisfaction, and they're a person for whom you feel empathy or respect, it's always good to listen, understand and capture their wisdom. But remember that it is *their* wisdom. Whatever you do – or don't – know about riding a bike, your obligation is to become an expert on your own life, to establish the style(s) of riding that suits your temperament and purposes.

WHEN IN DOUBT, LEAVE IT OUT

⊙⊙⊙

Cycling is simple. Unless you're racing in the woods or touring hard and heavy-laden over hilly country, you're unlikely to need three chainrings. A super-wide range of gears is mostly only useful to the sales force, who can confidently tell potential buyers, 'This one has the gears for you,' without asking about the potential buyer's intended journeys, fitness or even trying to explain what a gear actually is. Understandably, the seller is unlikely to reveal that the bike is also carrying quite a few gears the customer will probably never use.

Anything fitted on a pedal cycle has to be moved by the rider pushing the pedals. If you're in doubt about any facility, it's best to leave it off. There may be moments when you regret not having it. But all the rest of the time you'll be relieved not to be hauling it around. Extra features don't necessarily make things easier – they always mean more baggage.

WE ARE WHO
WE CHOOSE TO BE

⊙ ⊙ ⊙

Miguel Induráin is a notoriously taciturn man. Happy – as the cliché has it – to let his legs do the talking. As a practical farm boy, he chose cycle racing over soccer because, at the bike club, they fed you after training.

He won the Spanish National Road Race Championship in 1992, which entitled him to wear a special jersey, designed in the red and yellow of the Spanish flag. Induráin is a modest man and declined the honour.

Induráin's choice of jersey led to persistent speculation on his political beliefs. A controversy that left him – as usual – poker-faced and silent. Eventually, when asked directly to comment on the subject, he dismissed it thus: 'I was born in Navarre. I hold a Spanish passport. But I am, above all, a bicycle-racer.' This noble declaration, politically correct in the best sense, defines a modern version of identity. We all have manifest biographical details, but we are who we choose to be.

COURAGE IS NOT AN ABSENCE OF FEAR

Risk assessment is a key life skill. Complacency and underestimating hazards can have disastrous results – overcaution can mean missing out on fun.

Modern living often involves leaving risk assessment to strangers – products, vehicles, buildings, technology. We put our lives in the hands of others without considering the dangers. Ninety-five per cent of human history happened before agriculture. Our wild, prehistoric ancestors may have had some control of fire, tools made of wood, stone and bone, and even clay pots, but their world was full of danger and uncertainty. Being frightened is a natural human condition – we are natural-born risk assessors.

On a bicycle, difficulties and dangers tend to be clear, present and immediate. Bike riding is a practical study of risk assessment.

FIND A PARTNER TO ENJOY THE JOURNEY WITH

A tandem is mostly a luxury item because it needs two people going to the same place at the same time. The good news for such a duo is that a 'twicer' weighs less than two solos, staying close together is effortless and the machine's air resistance is not much more than a solo. These advantages mean the team's performance will be closer to that of the stronger rider.

On a classic tandem, the 'pilot' sits in front, connected to the second rider, the 'stoker', by a timing chain. The riders must pedal together. The stoker can't see the road ahead and has no independent control over their feet.

More comfortable configurations are available. For example, a design that puts the stoker in front in a recumbent position, with a better view, and a freewheel on the timing chain so they can coast at will. The pilot can see forward over the stoker. Their heads are close together for conversation.

SAFETY AND DANGER ARE THE SAME THING

The mechanic notices the plugs at the ends of the handlebars are missing, so selects a used wine cork from a drawer. She offers it to the open tube at one end of the bars, takes a knife and shaves the cork's end until it just fits in, whacks the cork further in with a rubber hammer and slices off almost all of what remains sticking out. Then she starts to do the same on the other side.

The teenage rider watching asks, 'What are you doing that for?'

'Well, imagine you had a crash, or just a silly fall, and landed on the hole at the end of the handlebar? It could hurt you badly – gouge your flesh like an apple corer. Once it's plugged it'll only give you a bruise.'

The rider's eyes widen slightly as the mechanic continues, 'The point of a bike is to be dangerous. Make it safer and you can be *more* dangerous, with *less* risk. Safety and danger are the same thing.'

CYCLISTS LIVE LONGER

⊙ ⊙ ⊙

A doctor suggests more exercise, so you go to the gym or start running around the park. Then your life changes – perhaps you have children or get more pressure from work. Your exercise regime comes under threat: you miss one week, then another, and the pattern is broken.

Construct a life where cycle travel is part of your everyday routine and you won't need to find time for exercise – the convenience of a bike for local journeys *saves* time. If life brings more stress, you will get a better workout when you're in a hurry. If a doctor says you need more exercise, then find a bar – or other attractive destination – at the top of a hill.

Mayer Hillman, the researcher who revealed that people who ride bikes live longer and typically enjoy the health of somebody ten years younger, summed it up nicely: 'Cycling is not a free lunch. It's a lunch you get paid to eat.'

BE PREPARED FOR ALL WEATHERS

Stage fifteen of the 1998 Tour de France crossed three towering passes to a ski-station finish. After a sunny start, the temperature dropped to 3 degrees Celsius (37 degrees Fahrenheit) in heavy rain. On the second pass, Bobby Julich noticed a rain jacket in the pocket of another rider and asked a teammate to go back to their car and fetch one for him.

The day is remembered for Italian Marco Pantani and his long-range solo attack, which won the stage and the Tour. Pantani broke away on the penultimate climb. At the top, he put on his long-sleeved jacket. Race favourite and 1996 winner Jan Ullrich only had a gilet. Ullrich held his gap behind Pantani steady on the chilling, 80-kilometre-per-hour (50-miles-per-hour) descent and along the last valley but 'cracked' on the final 9-kilometre (6-mile) climb and finished nine minutes behind the audacious Italian winner. Julich, however, lost four minutes to Pantani and held on to take third place when the Tour finished in Paris. It was the best Grand Tour place of his career.

HELPING OTHERS CAN BE SELFISH

Moving a bike is primarily about getting air that's in front of you behind you. Two competent riders cooperating can go with less effort than one. Keeping company has other advantages: a group need only carry one set of tools, can take turns to navigate and security is better, too. Comrades can also bring consolation.

Group travel also has costs. Companions may get on your nerves. Is working harder to keep up or going slower to allow them to stay with you justified by the benefits of their company?

This recurring question may come up in the planning of a long trip, on meeting a random stranger on the road or in a race or randonnée. 'Who is this person?' 'Will their presence make me more effective?' If 'yes', look after them. If not, let them go ahead or fall behind. Looking out for others and naked selfishness are not necessarily opposites – offering help to others can help you, too.

TRUST YOUR TEAMMATES

Bicycle road racing is a team endeavour: important wins rely on loyal comrades. In other sports, all members of a victorious team get matching medals. Road racing is more like 'real life' – everybody works hard then one gets star credit.

A support rider, or domestique, may fetch water or shelter a lead rider from wind resistance. If the leader has a puncture, they hand over their wheel, or bike – anything to conserve the protected rider's energy. A domestique-deluxe – a rider strong enough to stay with their leader in the hardest parts of the race – may go ahead early on so they're available to help when the star catches up.

A domestique may be content to suffer in the service of others, enjoying riding without the responsibility of delivering results. Others dream of personal glory. In strong teams, the leadership may be flexible, left open to see who's fittest as the race develops. Team politics may produce splits and treachery.

Good management and a swift recognition of internal conflicts are necessary. Successful teamwork comes from respect, openness and trust.

BECOME EXPERIENCED, THEN BE FRIVOLOUS

Drinking after a day's work, she noticed the park was filling up. 'Is it the Dunwich Dynamo tonight?' she asked the man handing out routing information. Eight hundred years ago, the North Sea port of Dunwich, England, was the same size as London. The capital grew while Dunwich was washed away. The Dynamo, a traditional night ride in July, runs 185 kilometres (115 miles) from London to the last seaside remnants of the lost city.

Wishing her friends goodnight, she went home, drank a pot of coffee and changed into cycling clothes. On the familiar route into the outer suburbs, she caught a group and slowed slightly, glad of the company. Later, she nursed them as they flagged. Chasing down red lights through the short summer night, crossing the countryside in the early morning chill and feeling the old roads gathering towards an important place, she hit the beach just as the day got warm.

Become experienced and build your confidence: it will allow you to be frivolous when necessary.

CHANGE THE WORLD WHEN YOU HAVE TO

Jo Roach is the mother of a daughter with a learning disability. She became a raffle-ticket seller, jumble-sale helper, school governor, fundraiser and, in her fifties, a qualified cycle trainer, all in aid of her daughter's cause.

Jo's daughter had no problem learning to cycle, and they looked for a club to help her continue as an adult. In 2002, clubs were for racing or long-distance riding, and mainly run by men. Somebody suggested Jo start a club for adults with learning disabilities. In 2004, the all-ability cycle club 'Pedal Power' became her second baby.

Now Pedal Power has a fleet of bikes and tricycles, solos and tandems, to suit all kinds of riders. Its membership includes adults and children with a disability, their family members, carers and anyone else interested in fun on wheels. Jo explains, 'They say "It takes a village to raise a child." It takes dedicated volunteers and enthusiastic members for a club to thrive.'

WE'RE ALL ONLY BORROWING IT

On 8 July 2004, stage five of the Tour de France, Amiens to Chartres, was characterized by windy weather and multiple crashes. A breakaway group of five escaped the chaos and finished twelve minutes ahead of the pack, moving the quintet into the top five positions on the General Classification (GC), pushing previous leader, Lance Armstrong, down to sixth.

For 100 years, the GC leader had been identified by the yellow jersey. To wear one, even for one day, is a rare honour, the highlight of many careers.

The following day the new 'yellow jersey' – young Thomas Voeckler – remarked to Armstrong, 'Don't worry, I'm only borrowing it.'

Armstrong, not renowned for humility, replied, 'We're all only borrowing it.'

The GC is ranked by time. Cycle travel keeps you close to the brutal realities of wind, hills, hours, minutes, seconds … mortality. The universe is indifferent to your status and achievements. We're all only borrowing it.

GOOD IDEAS DON'T HAVE TO REPLACE OLD IDEAS

Pedalling is pushing down on the front pedal. Every 180 degrees, there's a 'dead spot' where one pedal is exactly above the other – you can't push either and have to turn them instead. On fixed-gear bikes, while the cycle rolls, the pedals move. You can't 'coast' to rest your legs while you're moving so there's no dead spot. Once you are moving, you don't have to pedal; you only need to speed up the pedals as they fly around. The bike pedals you.

Bikes with freewheels, an automatic clutch that enables coasting, became available in 1898. By the late twentieth century, the only 'valid' uses for fixed-gear bikes were velodrome racing or acrobatic cycling.

Some individuals have always chosen fixed-gear for simplicity, economy and efficiency. Early in the twenty-first century, the internet brought these thrifty minimalists together and a global 'fixie' craze followed. The fad passed, but fixed gear is, once again, a legitimate choice for travel. Not everything old-fashioned is useless.

MAKE FRIENDS WITH PAIN AND DISAPPOINTMENT

In 2008, Nicole Cooke crowned her stellar career by becoming the first rider to win Olympic and World Championship road races in the same season. She was also the first Briton to win the Tour de France. She used her prestige to denounce doping culture. Racing for men survived the scandals of the early twenty-first century. Women's racing – a newer phenomenon whose sponsorship base relied on a healthy image – suffered much more.

She described her national federation as 'run by men for men'. Often frustrated by lack of support, Nicole tended to overtrain, raced nursing damaged knees and lost some of her prime years convalescing from surgery.

Cooke retired at twenty-nine; in a different time and place she may have raced longer and won more. But life is a one-way street. In her autobiography, she thanks her competitors and rivals for spurring her on. Pain and disappointment are unavoidable, and essential to illuminate the good times.

KIT SAVES MONEY

Making bicycles the mainstay of your transport economy is easier if you have capital to invest and storage space for multiple machines. Creative thinking helps. A quality folding bike can be expensive, but their one-size-fits-all potential makes them easy to sell on if you ever want to. They store in small spaces. Similarly, a flatbed bike trailer with detachable wheels can disappear under a bed if needed.

When expecting a guest arriving by mass transit, without a bike, lash your folding bike on the trailer, pack a book and spin out to the airstrip, bus stop or rail station. When the visitor arrives, unfold the bike, tie their luggage to the trailer and ride home together. When it's time for them to leave, reverse the process, minus the book.

Depending on your relationship, the guest may drop the equivalent of two taxi rides into your bike paraphernalia fund.

BREAK DOWN COMPLEX PROBLEMS INTO SIMPLE ONES

A novice cyclist may watch a busy traffic environment and wonder, 'How can I fit into that chaos?'

To share space comfortably with other road users, you need skills in three areas. Firstly, the ability to manage a bike to a minimum standard: stop, start, steer, look behind and ride one-handed to give bold and confident hand signals. All this without conscious thought as you concentrate on what the other people are planning to do next.

Then you need to understand the formalities of 'traffic' in the locality. What people expect you to do and what you can expect from them. Almost everyone is doing what they think they're supposed to be doing, almost all of the time. You can spot a transgressor coming from far away. The system has to be simple: stupid people need to understand it.

The third requirement is the presence to communicate and negotiate with others. This final piece of the jigsaw is supported by your confidence in the first two. If any element is missing, you may have trouble.

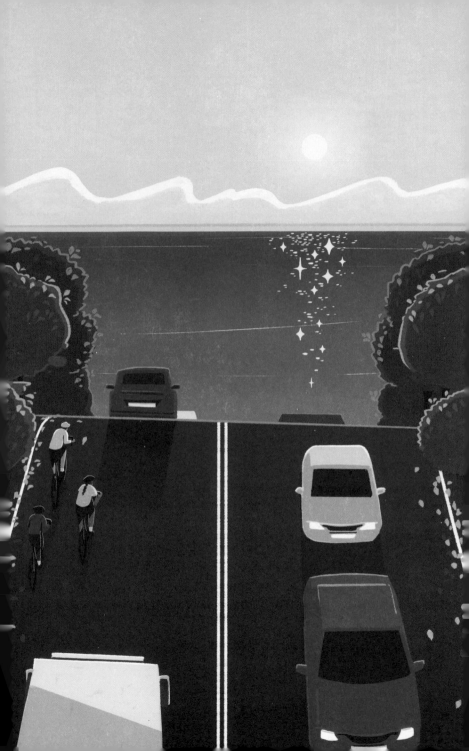

HAVE ROLE MODELS, NOT HEROES

Lance Armstrong, a boy swimmer from Texas, was a professional triathlete at sixteen and won the 1993 bicycle road race World Championship aged twenty-two. After surviving life-threatening cancer, he rebuilt his swimmer's body lighter.

Perhaps focused by the brush with mortality, he won the Tour de France seven years straight then retired to concentrate on his cancer charity. The 'miracle' comeback spread Lance's popularity beyond cycling.

Several important support riders tested positive for doping after leaving Armstrong's team and other circumstantial evidence fuelled persistent rumours. Eventually revelations from former teammates forced Armstrong to confess to years of systematic cheating. Angry ex-fans denounced him as an evil fraud.

Others who'd watched his career more sceptically understood he is both villain and victim. 'Scientific preparation', or doping, was rife in professional bike racing and Armstrong had organized his medical programme with detailed efficiency. If you never adored him as a saint, you don't need to hate him now.

TRAVEL LIKE A MILLIONAIRE TRAMP

You wake in the dark, the impromptu camp hidden from a mountain road. There's no building for miles and no passing traffic but you want to get moving before dawn. It's daylight by the time the bikes are packed and up on the carriageway. A site inspection confirms you've left no trace. At the first river, swim and brew coffee in the sunshine.

After dark that evening, at a boutique hotel in a big historic city, a lift from the basement garage brings you to a room equipped with a hot-water bath and thick towels. Damp sleeping bags are draped on designer furniture, then you wash and change for late-night sightseeing. The next morning, a lavish buffet sets you up for another day on the road.

If funds permit, you can live like millionaires every day; with less cash, subsist like vagrants. Adjust the blend to suit your budget and use the contrast to relish the joys of both.

DON'T WASTE MONEY ON CHEAP TOOLS

C ompared to such complex items as cars or computers, pedal cycles are simple. The computer will be obsolete in a few years and the cheap car worn out in twenty. Yet a pedal cycle, with its strictly limited power source, engineered with greater precision – like an aeroplane, race car or musical instrument – will stand the test of time.

The service life of a bicycle is measured in decades not years. If a bike is specified for economical operation, the running costs can also be very low. Choose a bicycle that fits your purpose, ride it, change the moving parts when necessary, mention it in your will. And don't waste money on cheap tools.

CARRY LESS THAN YOU NEED

Unless you're going into wilderness or on a road where settlements are far apart, you don't have to carry everything you might need. Where people are living, the essentials will be available. A personal luxury or two are worth more than the everyday stuff you can buy in any town.

If your route takes you over highlands, where you may need extra clothes, find a charity shop in the last valley town and buy an extra layer. Donate surplus garments at another thrift store in the first town you reach on the other side. They can wait there for you – or someone else – going the other way.

In a country without charity shops, find used clothes or cheap new clothes in markets. If they're worth it, you can easily give them away on the other side. Carrying less stuff is always a good idea. Practical, commonplace interactions with locals can also be a pleasure.

CELEBRATE DIVERSITY

Modern culture tends to see earning, spending and owning as our most important functions. Gaining satisfaction from riding a bike, which is free at the point of delivery, is interpreted by some as an economic blasphemy.

To avoid being associated with a rebel 'out group', some people hyphenate themselves: 'I'm a mountain-biker.' 'I'm an urban-cyclist.' 'I'm a racing-cyclist.' They may even denounce others, vainly trying to avoid being taken for 'one of those people'. 'They're not proper cyclists because…

… they're too slow/fast.

… they wear/don't wear special clothes.

… they wear/don't wear proper shoes.

… their bikes are too dirty/clean/cheap/expensive.'

Sigmund Freud called this foolishness 'the narcissism of small differences'. Envious people who claim to hate cyclists don't recognize such distinctions. Whatever the exact terms of your current habits or interests, don't be shy. Celebrate our diversity. There is strength in unity.

TEST THE WATER FIRST

○ · ○ · ○

It's wise to leave a generous margin for error. Caution is prudent, good judgement and quick thinking are efficient. The 'reckless twin' technique can help sharpen your decision-making.

Imagine you're waiting to turn on to a busy road, calculating two gaps in the speeding traffic, the first to cross the nearer lane, the second to turn into the further. It makes sense to be conservative, not to change your 'risk thermostat' just because you've been waiting a while or there are people waiting behind you. When you see a possible opportunity to make your move, but decide there's not enough time and space, send an imaginary 'reckless twin' ahead, and consider how they get on. You may find there's more space than you thought. Repeated pondering on the progress of a cheeky doppelgänger will improve your judgement.

OWN YOUR IGNORANCE

How long does it take to learn to ride a bike? I don't know. I've never met anyone who can. This answer may be annoying but is not necessarily untrue.

Christopher Froome was born in Africa, far from the historic heartlands of cycle sport, yet forced his way to its top. He's won multiple Grand Tours and, unlike other noted serial victors, has tested negative at all medical controls or passed later on appeal. On a reconnaissance ride in 2019, he tried to blow his nose going downhill and ended up in intensive care with multiple fractures. If he knew how to ride a bike, how did that happen? If Chris Froome can't, we've got no chance.

Confidently explaining you can't is vanity disguised as modesty: 'I'll never get to the mountaintop but may have some idea where the foothills lie.' Learning cycling is not a task to be completed; it's an open-ended process of self-discovery to be enjoyed.

ENJOY THE WORLD WITHOUT SPOILING IT

☉ ☉ ☉

Finding a vacation destination full of local character, undiscovered by tourists, is a persistent fantasy of the modern world. If you can get there without effort, risk of danger or risk of boredom, then it's likely to be full of people just like yourself.

A cycle tourist passes through places that don't feature in guidebooks, where the only tourists are in airliners high overhead or on buses whizzing round the ring road. Spend an evening in a town where the most significant buildings are a sausage factory and a linseed oil refinery and you're likely to meet locals interested in you, not just what's in your wallet. When you get to the honeypot destinations, the time spent in undistinguished spots will help you deal with the tourist hustle.

No matter who they are or where they come from, people who arrive on bikes – like common labourers – only need food, drink and shelter. Cycle touring allows you to enrich the country you are passing through without distorting its landscape or economy.

AUTONOMY IS PRECIOUS

An image of Hiram Maxim's first success – an 1897 motorized tricycle package-carrier – looks strangely familiar. Its scale prefigures the light electric vehicles of the 2020s. The pedals were for starting the engine and added extra power up hills.

The latest battery boom – from high-performance supercars to air-tyred skateboards – helpfully reminds people that pedal cycles and automobiles are not opposites. They're parts of the same project.

Battery-assisted pedal cycles are popular. Their modern promoters encourage the illusion that they're *only* a benefit. Electricity is not a source of energy; it's a means of storing and transmitting energy. Vehicles that use motive force from a power station, via a lithium battery, reduce a rider's immediate workload. When the charge is all gone, they impose a heavy penalty.

There may be good reasons to cross the line from running on coffee and cake to relying on remote, complicated systems. The costs are less spontaneity, less autonomy and more worry.

VIGILANT MANAGEMENT AVOIDS DISTRESS

○○○

For an experienced rider, the important interface is not between animal and machine; it's where the tyres kiss the road. Monitoring the machine's condition and checking your body is one task.

Some feelings demand attention. Correct a wrinkle in your sock before it rubs a blister that'll hurt tomorrow. Other pains that can be safely managed are not an attack from outside – don't try to ignore them. You are the pain. Savour, occupy, dissolve it from the inside.

Noise when you go over a bump suggests a fitting – for example, a luggage rack – is loose. Noise while you pedal or freewheel suggest a problem with the wheels or brakes. This is worth stopping to check. Noise only when you pedal suggest a problem with the drive. Does the noise sound in all gears? Or only when you push hard?

Novices tend to ignore their bikes: 'It's working. I won't think about it.' This leads to distressing surprises. Vigilance and active management work better.

SOME PROBLEMS HAVE NO SOLUTIONS

A new bicycle chain is 98 per cent efficient. It doesn't get hot or make a noise; it pulls. The metal-on-metal movement of its links requires lubrication. Lubrication must be sticky to stay in place; because it's sticky, it picks up dirt.

For a chain that runs in one position, a chain case is a good answer. In this clean, dry environment, a chain can last 100 years, but a chain case makes rear-wheel punctures more complicated. Chains designed for modern gear systems – with nine, ten or eleven sprockets on the rear wheel – wear out quickly. Their factory lubrication can last until they need replacing.

Don't lubricate a chain until it squeaks. Clean off as much contaminated lubricant as you can before adding more, meanly. Then wipe off as much as possible. Excess lubricant mixes with sharp dust, making a paste that grinds down moving parts.

If you find keeping your chain lubricated *and* clean troublesome, it's not your fault. Some problems have no solution.

SET GOALS AND STICK TO THEM

As a music student in Boston, Ayesha 'Quick Brown Fox' McGowan got a bike to get around. She enjoyed the freedom. It improved her access to employment and released her from the cost, frustration and discomfort of public transport.

In the excitement of the twenty-first century's internet-driven bike boom, the cycling bug bit her. She took up road racing in 2014 and in her third event won a state championship. Finding cycle sport an almost exclusively white affair, she stated her ambition to become the first ever African-American woman professional bike racer.

A prolific networker, with a popular presence on social media, McGowan also dedicates herself to increasing the representation and participation of women of colour in all kinds of cycling. In 2020, she signed her first professional contract with Liv Racing. She quickly went on to win the League of American Bicyclists' inaugural 'Kittie Knox Award' as a champion of equality, diversity and inclusion.

RESPECT YOUR SURROUNDINGS

Bikes can fit in on busy roads designed for fast motor traffic as well as along paths shared with the informal patterns of people on foot. Where those around you are enclosed in heavy machinery, it's imperative they notice your presence. As the pilot of a light, unstable vehicle you have the potential to move sideways more quickly than anyone else. Practise generating charismatic power, but without anger.

Motor-free space, where you're the scariest element in the mix, requires a different persona. It's not just that you must not put others in danger; you must not put them in fear, either. Don't hurry in spaces shared with 'soft traffic', don't assume everyone has good vision or good hearing, and don't assume that others will control their unpredictable animals or toddlers.

The role of the bike rider is to take the conviviality of the park out on to the highway and not to bring the threatening temper of motor traffic into walking spaces.

SNIFF OUT THE FEET OF ANCESTORS

Old-time navigation meant rolling into town on a road named after a place behind you, such as the 'Rue de Paris', crossing a river bridge near a big church and market square, then exiting up a street identified by a settlement ahead, such as the 'Rue de Rouen'.

For pilgrims now, it's more complicated. New roads don't connect places – they avoid them. As you reach a city's limits, direction signs for your onward objective are likely to send you round a bleak orbital. The signs to follow are in the *centre ville* category.

Long-ago conflicts produced some towns deliberately isolated from through traffic. Some old tracks have been blocked by railways or canals. Ignoring signs doesn't always work. When it does, you follow a straighter line, passing downtown bakeries, bistros, bike shops and fruiterers.

The ancestors who defined old paths and sited ancient bridges wanted to walk, ride ponies, roll barrows and drive livestock on the shortest, flattest routes. Practise sniffing them out.

ABOUT THE AUTHOR

PATRICK FIELD founded the London School of Cycling (LSC) in 1993 with the insane intention of teaching adults to use pedal bikes. He has authored a number of cycling guidebooks focused on London and its environs, including *Breathing Spaces* (1993), *Get Lost* (1994), *Cycle London* (2011) and *London on Two Wheels* (2015), and contributed to the anthology *Autopia* (2002). He has also written for *New Cyclist*, *Cycling Today*, *Cycling Plus* and *Cycle* magazines. Patrick continues to run the LSC and is a founder of the legendary Dunwich Dynamo.

ABOUT THE ILLUSTRATOR

HARRY GOLDHAWK is an illustrator and pattern designer based in Newlyn, UK. He takes his inspiration from the natural world around him. Harry studied illustration at the University of Gloucestershire, where he started his illustrated gifts and stationery business, Papio Press, with his wife and fellow illustrator Zanna Goldhawk.